TABLE OF CON

PROLOGUE

'In the paradoxical revolution that we are still experiencing, we've been building the game closer to our own penalty area in order to attack better. And more and more, we've gotten closer to the opposite penalty area in order to defend better'.

Emiliano Battazzi

I think this quote correctly presents the main theme of this book: to analyze, codify, and explore, from theory to practice, one of the fundamental principles of modern football, which is building the game from the back.

The first decade of the new millennium brought us a gift: Pep Guardiola's revolution at FC Barcelona. A transformation that had its roots in Arrigo Sacchi's Milan and in the Dutch "Total Football" of Rinus Michels, Johan Cruyff, and Louis van Gaal (to name a few), with the spasmodic search for possession and control of the ball, space and time.

Here, building from the back has become the starting point towards proactive and non-speculative football, aiming to achieve victory through collective play. If we believe that this style of play should be a reference point for our first teams, then there is no doubt that it's even more important for the development of our young players.

Davide Zenorini, an attentive student of tactical innovations in recent years, provides us with a clear, simple, and practical view of the subject because, as Cruyff says, 'playing soccer is simple, but playing simple soccer is the most difficult thing there is'.

Antonio Gagliardi
UEFA Pro License Coach
Italian National Team Analyst

INTRODUCTION

In modern football we often talk about the "building of the game". In this book we will delve deep and analyze different possibilities for building from the back, starting the action from the goalkeeper.

We will start with a tactical scheme that uses the 4-3-3 or 4-2-3-1 as a reference in the possession phase, but these ideas will be highly adaptable to any other system that you wish to use with your team. I firmly believe that regardless of the tactical system, it's the principles that make the difference. By choosing these principles, in relation to our game model, we will reveal our team's true potential.

The situations that we are going to analyze are suitable for those who wish to impart a modern vision of football, helping their players understand how to build the game and create a strong collective identity. This idea of football is based on one fundamental maxim: the desire to possess the ball.

To have effective results when building the game, we must have more options to escape our opponents, find spaces to attack, and score goals. To do this, it's necessary to study how the opponent pressures us during our buildout and train collective movements (rotations) that are well codified and recognizable to our players; decide how many players will participate in the buildout; maintain possession in order to "move" the opponents so we can destabilize their defensive balance and attack them where we find the right gap at the right time; have goalkeepers who are committed to "play out" with their feet, through situational exercises; Build out long when the opponents seek to recover up high; advancing with the ball, conquering the field of play with coordinated patterns divided into three phases (the starting phase, the consolidation phase, and the conclusion or finishing phase).

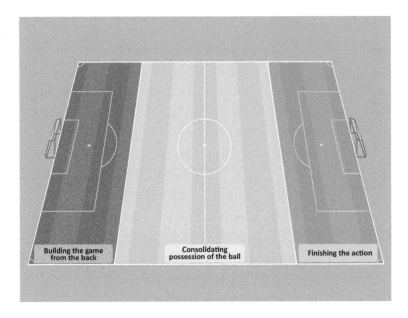

Dividing the field for the building of the game.

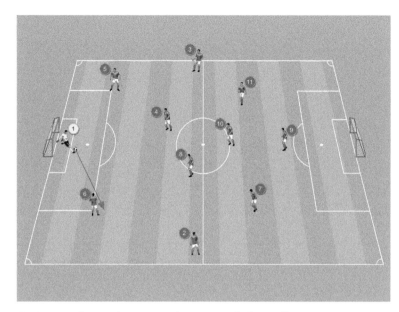

Basic tactical setup for starting the game with the goalkeeper in possession.

CHAPTER 1
GAME MODEL

My opinion is that in modern football it's essential to design our game model according to the characteristics of our players. If we have a team predisposed to play with short and quick passes in tight spaces, we can apply a very precise model. If, on the other hand, we have players who prefer to play vertically due to their specific individual characteristics, that adaptation must be made.

In any case, it will be necessary to study and analyze how we can attack our opponents by building the action from the back. Sharing the general principles with your team at the beginning of the season can be of great help to the players. Making them responsible for decision-making and encouraging them to use their natural qualities according to the game situation being faced is a recommendable path for their individual growth.

Simple and clear objectives should be established for each training session. The most important thing is to find the right approach for reaching them. An excellent solution could be to create continuous personal and collective challenges while maintaining a constant focus on improving fitness as well as technique and tactics.

Building the game from the back allows a team to grow in personality and generate more favorable conditions for putting their opponents in difficulty, so training this ability is very useful for improving our teams.

14

DEFENSIVE TRANSITION

OFFENSIVE ORGANIZATION

DEFENSIVE ORGANIZATION

OFFENSIVE TRANSITION

CHAPTER 2
DIDACTICS AND PRINCIPALS OF BUILDING THE GAME

2.1 INITIAL POSITION OF THE GOALKEEPER AND THE FOUR DEFENDERS

In this illustration we see the basic structure for building the game through the goalkeeper.

When the goalkeeper receives the ball, the two centerbacks (5 and 6) spread out to create passing lines in the corners of the penalty area. The two outside backs (2 and 3) provide maximum width and seek  to reach midfield in order to offer the goalkeeper the possibility of looking for a pass further up the field.

For the coach:

- The body position of the players must be oriented towards the ball/opponent's goal.

2.2 INITIAL STRUCTURE OF THE THREE CENTRAL MIDFIELDERS

The three midfielders (4, 8 and 10) play central roles and are at the heart of the building of the game. Moving in a coordinated and dynamic way, they create a triangular shape in order to find the space and passing lines to receive directly from the goalkeeper (1) or one of the centerbacks (5 and 6).

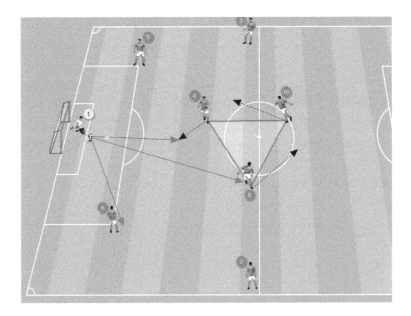

For the coach:

- The body position of the players must be oriented towards the ball/opponent's goal.
- The correct distances must be maintained: using the corners of the goalkeeper's box for the centerbacks, the midfield line for

the outside backs, and maintaining a distance of approximately 12-15 meters between each of the midfielders, according to the location of the ball and teammates.

- Once the goalkeeper directs the play to the centerback (6), this player's reception starts a midfield rotation that seeks to occupy spaces with the correct timing.
- If the goalkeeper chooses to play to the defensive midfielder (4), the rotation will be managed mainly by the two inside players (8 and 10) who will be ready to receive the ball.
- It's important to play the passes with the proper weight.

2.3 COORDINATED ROTATIONAL MOVEMENT OF THE CENTRAL MIDFIELDERS

The rotation of the three central midfielders (4, 8 and 10) is used to create continuous passing lines in search of a free-man situation that will allow us to play. We will create a small playing area in front of the defenders that will allow the goalkeeper to choose the best option for building the action and, at the same time, reach the consolidation of possession zone with the intention of attacking in the most effective and organized manner. In this way, once the rotation has been carried out, two midfielders (4 and 10) will provide greater coverage to the two centerbacks in the event that the ball is lost.

For the coach:

- The body position of the players must be oriented towards the ball/opponent's goal.
- The correct distances must be maintained: only two staggered midfielders can enter the rectangle, and their bodies must be profiled to play vertically as the first option.
- If the goalkeeper plays to the centerback (6), the closest midfielder (4) must move to try and free up the space to find the opposite midfielder (10) on the move, while the other (8) looks for depth and to prolong the action.
- If the goalkeeper chooses to play to the defensive midfielder (4), the other two midfielders will have to leave that rectangle to occupy space in depth.
- It's important to play the passes with the proper weight.

2.4 FROM BUILDING THE GAME FROM THE BACK TO THE CONSOLIDATION OF POSSESSION

Having built the game from the back, our objective will be to consolidate possession of the ball in the central area of the pitch and find the most effective way to score. Maintaining the dynamism and the triangular shape of the midfielders, we must look for movements from the attackers that will allow us to finish.

In this case, after building the game from the back with the goalkeeper (1) and rotating to avoid the opponent's pressing, the midfielders (4, 8 and 10) look for the winger (11) who can then lay the ball off to the inside player (10). This will create a superiority in the left channel where the outside back (3) can finish the action.

For the coach:

- The body position of the players must be oriented towards the ball/opponent's goal.
- The correct distances must be maintained, creating geometric shapes with correct spacing (depending on the position of theball and teammates) between the midfielders to try and gain forward territory.

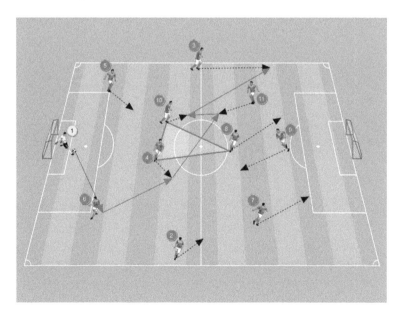

- When the midfielder (4) begins to set up the movement after receiving from the centerback (6), the center forward (9) must move closer while the midfielder (8) attacks space, or vice versa.
- It's important to play the passes with the proper weight.

2.5 OPTIMAL OCCUPATION OF SPACE

To consolidate possession we will have to get used to mentally dividing the field into five parts so that the outside backs (2 and 3) are not in the same channel as the wingers (7 and 11). This is done to have more passing lines and, above all, to functionally occupy the entire width of the field of play. When exchanging positions, try to maintain the triangle in order to have support during the possession phase and have preventative coverage in case the ball is lost (green triangle).

For the coach:

- The body position of the players must be oriented towards the ball/opponent's goal.

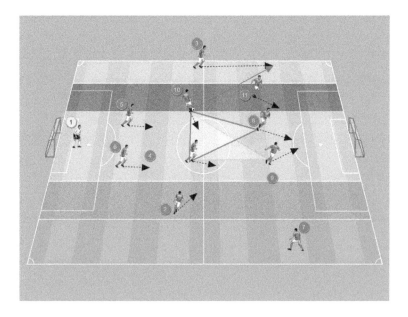

- It's important that the outside backs and the wingers are never in the same channel.
- The correct distances must be maintained depending on the channel and the position of the ball and teammates: when the winger (11) frees up space in the outside lane with an inward

movement, the midfielder (10) has to find the outside back pushing up (3) and then provide coverage.

- One midfielder must go to complete the action (8) while another provides coverage (4).
- It's important to play the passes with the proper weight.

2.6 CREATING A HIGHER DENSITY OF PLAYERS IN THE CENTRAL MIDFIELD ZONE

There are several possibilities for creating density (putting more players) in the center of the field. One option is to slide the two outside backs (2 and 3) into the middle to act as central players. For an action that involves the defensive midfielder (4) in possession and between the center backs, the wingers (7 and 11) shall provide maximum width in the outside channels and the center forward (9) provides maximum depth in the middle. In this case, space is freed up in the two inside channels where the two attacking midfielders (8 and 10) can operate. The two outside backs (2 and 3) shift inwardly to act as new midfielders and provide support and coverage in the middle of the pitch. In the event that possession is lost, the outside backs move diagonally towards the outermost channels. The midfield triangle (red) is created by the defensive midfielder (4) and the attacking midfielders (8 and 10). The same shape, for eventual preventative coverage, is always formed by the defensive midfielder (4) and the outside backs (2 and 3).

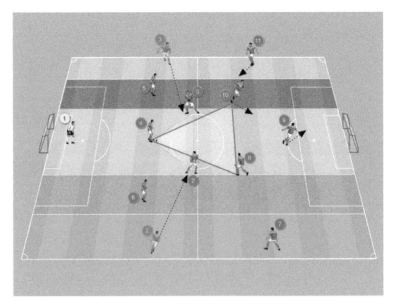

For the coach:

- The body position of the players must be oriented towards the ball/opponent's goal.
- It's important that the outside backs and the wingers are never in the same channel.
- The correct distances must be maintained depending on the channel and the position of the ball and teammates: the outside backs (2 and 3) slide when the midfielder (4) receives from the goalkeeper to build play from the back.
- If both outside backs decide to move and play in the central channel, they must do it together with synchronized movements.
- In the event of a loss of possession, it's essential for the outside backs (2 and 3) to make quick diagonal movements to the outer channels and for the two attacking midfielders (8 and 10) to drop into the central zone.
- It's important to play the passes with the proper weight.

2.7 FROM THE CONSOLIDATION OF POSSESSION TO FINISHING THROUGH THE WIDE CHANNELS

Once possession is established in the central area, you must look to finish the action quickly and effectively. Finding space in the wide channels is an alternative to attacking directly down the middle. By moving the ball, you will attempt to gain advanced territory and move and disrupt the opposing defense. The centerback (5) looks for space with a pass to the defensive midfielder (4) in the central zone, who plays vertically for the advanced attacking midfielder (8), who in turn lays the ball off to the outside back (2) who has moved into the middle. Then, with a wide delivery to the outermost channel, space is found to exploit the width of the field and the winger (7) crosses for the finish. The triangle is maintained in the center of the field, in this case formed by the defensive midfielder (4) and the attacking midfielders (8 and 10), with an identical shape that serves to provide preventative coverage for a possible loss of possession composed of the defensive midfielder (4) and the outside backs (2 and 3).

For the coach:

- The body position of the players must be oriented towards the ball/opponent's goal.
- It's important that the outside backs and the wingers are never in the same channel.
- The correct distances must be maintained depending on the channel and the position of the ball and teammates: the outside backs (2 and 3) slide when the midfielder (4) receives from the goalkeeper to build play from the back.
- If both outside backs decide to move and play in the central channel, they must do it together with synchronized movements.
- The team must always keep a player in the outermost channel in order to have space to play, look for one-vs-one's, and open

up the opposing defensive line to enable forward runs from the midfielders.

- It's important to play the passes with the proper weight.

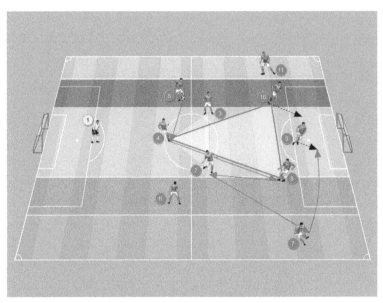

2.8 FROM THE CONSOLIDATION OF POSSESSION TO FINISHING THROUGH THE CENTRAL CHANNELS

Another way to finish quickly and effectively is to find space in the central channels and attack the opponent directly. Looking to play quickly with longer passes to a teammate can create different alternatives for arriving and finishing. The centerback (5) makes a pass to the defensive midfielder (4), who seeks to lay the ball off to the other defender (6). This time, the outside backs (2 and 3) decide to play in the outermost channels. The centerback (6) in possession plays vertically to the center forward (9), who then plays to the attacking midfielder (8), who looks to assist the other midfielder (10) with a through ball after dismarking into space.

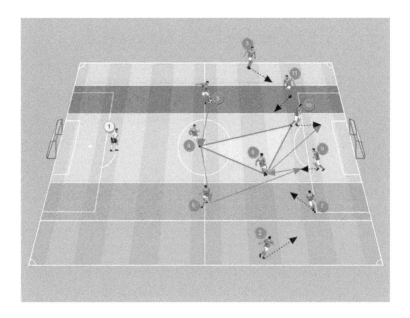

For the coach:

- The body position of the players must be oriented towards the ball/opponent's goal.

- The correct distances must be maintained depending on the channel and the position of the ball and teammates: the movement of the center forward (9) begins when the centerback (6) is about to receive the ball.

- When the centerback (6) makes it clear that he is looking to play vertically towards the center forward (9), the attacking midfielder behind the attacker (8) has to show in support in order to activate the forward run of the other attacking midfielder (10).

- It's important that the outside backs and the wingers are never in the same channel.

- Provide maximum width: always put players in the two outside channels to attack space without the ball.

- It's important to play the passes with the proper weight.

2.9 2.9 BUILDING THE GAME LONG THROUGH THE WINGER

When the opponent presses high, building the game with a long pass can be a valid alternative to get out of our half of the field. If moving the ball with the help of the goalkeeper becomes difficult due to the opponent's efforts, you may have to look to play directly towards the winger or the forward, who will provide you with depth and allow you to find free spaces.

In this case the outside back (3) drops the ball back to the centerback (5), who in turn plays it to the goalkeeper (1) who, because he cannot build from the back after he receives the ball, plays a long pass for the winger (7) to control in the finishing zone.

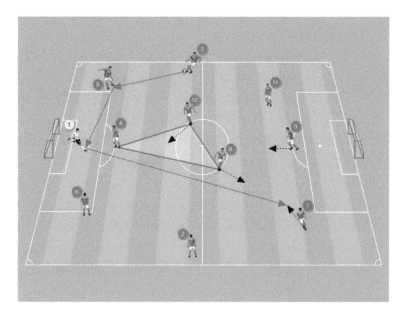

For the coach:

- The body position of the players must be oriented towards the ball/opponent's goal.
- Maintain the correct distances to achieve maximum width and maximum depth in order to have space to play.

- When the attackers (7, 9, and 11) recognize the difficulties of playing out of the back, they must be ready to receive a long ball to preserve the continuity of play and start an offensive action.
- The players without the ball must attack space.
- The wingers must try to receive and control the ball, trying to attack one-vs-one if possible. If they are marked, they can opt to direct a header to the center forward attacking in depth or look for support from the attacking midfielder (8).
- Once the long ball has been played, the team must shrink to win space in the opponent's half of the field as quickly as possible.
- The midfielders (4, 8 and 10) must maintain a triangular shape with distances between them that will be useful for the ball and the rest of the team, since they have to be ready to support the play.
- It's important to play the passes with the proper weight.

2.10 BUILDING THE GAME LONG THROUGH THE CENTER FORWARD

In this case the outside back (3) drops the ball back to the centerback (5), who plays it back to the goalkeeper (1), who receives the ball and passes it to the other defender (6). This player is unable to build from the back and looks to play a long ball towards the center forward (9) in the finishing zone.

For the coach:

- The body position of the players must be oriented towards the ball/opponent's goal.
- Maintain the correct distances to achieve maximum width and maximum depth in order to have space to play.
- When the attackers (7, 9, and 11) recognize the difficulties of playing out of the back, they must be ready to receive a long ball to preserve the continuity of play and start an offensive action.

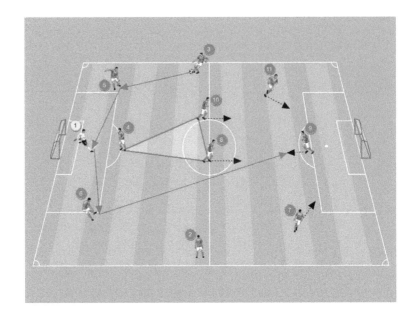

- The center forward (9) receives the long ball and, as the first option, he must think about controlling it and keeping it while his teammates move up the field. Otherwise, he can look for the wingers (7 and 11) or lay the ball off to one of the supporting attacking midfielders. (8 and 10).
- Once the long ball has been played, the team must shrink to win space in the opponent's half of the field as quickly as possible.
- The midfielders (4, 8 and 10) must maintain a triangular shape with distances between them that are useful for the ball and the rest of the team, since they have to be ready to support the play.
- It's important to play the passes with the proper weight.

CHAPTER 3
BUILDING OUT FROM THE BACK

3.1 BUILDING OUT FROM THE BACK AGAINST AN OPPONENT WHO PRESSURES THE DEFENSIVE MIDFIELDER

Starting the buildout from the goalkeeper (1), the two centerbacks (5 and 6) must open up. The defensive midfielder (4) must try to attract the marking of the opponent (9) with a curved movement, creating a one-vs-one and freeing up space for the defender (5) to build out.

For the coach:

- Actively involve the goalkeeper in the building of the game.
- Correct body profile in an offensive direction.
- The first touch should facilitate building out from the back.
- Preventative coverage is important: once the ball leaves the defensive zone, the centerbacks must push their line up towards the middle of the field.

3.2 BUILDING OUT FROM THE BACK AGAINST AN OPPONENT WHO PRESSURES THE CENTERBACK

Starting the buildout from the goalkeeper (1), the two centerbacks (5 and 6) must open up. If the opponent (9) presses one of them (6), it becomes a one-vs-one and creates space to build out through the middle. With a curved movement, the defensive midfielder (4) can progress after receiving the ball from the goalkeeper (1).

For the coach:

- Actively involve the goalkeeper in the building of the game.
- Correct body profile in an offensive direction.
- The first touch should facilitate building out from the back.
- Preventative coverage is important: once the ball leaves the defensive zone, the centerbacks must push their line up towards the middle of the field.

3.3 BUILDING OUT FROM THE BACK AGAINST TWO OPPONENTS WHO PRESSURE THE CENTERBACKS

Starting the buildout from the goalkeeper (1), the two centerbacks (5 and 6) must open up as before, trying to "attract" the two rival attackers (Red 9 and 11) to the outside of the field to create one-vs-ones in the areas highlighted by the red circles. In addition, the outside backs (2 and 3) move up to midfield to provide width and depth. In this way, space is generated in the central channel where the defensive midfielder (4) makes a curved movement, preparing to receive with the body oriented towards the opposing goal.

For the coach:

- Actively involve the goalkeeper in the building of the game.
- Correct body profile in an offensive direction.
- The first touch should facilitate building out from the back.
- Pay attention to the timing of the play, maintaining the correct distances between channels and occupying space in a functional and effective way.
- Preventative coverage is important: once the ball leaves the defensive zone, the centerbacks must push their line up towards the middle of the field.

3.4 BUILDING OUT FROM THE BACK AGAINST AN OPPONENT WHO PRESSURES THE CENTERBACK AND THE DEFENSIVE MIDFIELDER

Starting the buildout from the goalkeeper (1), the two centerbacks (5 and 6) must open up, trying to "attract" the two rival attackers (9 and 11). In addition, the outside backs (2 and 3) move up to the midfield to provide width and depth. This time, as we can see, a forward (11) decides to go and close the goalkeeper's passing line to the defensive midfielder (4). This opens up space in the outside channel and the teams seeks to build out through the free defender (6).

For the coach:

- Actively involve the goalkeeper in the building of the game.
- Correct body profile in an offensive direction.
- The first touch should facilitate building out from the back.

- Pay attention to the timing of the play, maintaining the correct distances between channels and occupying space in a functional and effective way.
- Preventative coverage is important: once the ball leaves the defensive zone, the centerbacks must push their line up towards the middle of the field.

3.5 BUILDING OUT FROM THE BACK AGAINST THREE OPPONENTS WHO PRESSURE THE CENTERBACKS AND THE DEFENSIVE MIDFIELDER

Starting the buildout from the goalkeeper (1), the two centerbacks (5 and 6) must open up, trying to "attract" the two rival attackers (9 and 11). In addition, the outside backs (2 and 3) move up to the midfield to provide width and depth. The center forward (9) takes on our defensive midfielder (4), so it's necessary to seek numerical superiority in the midfield with the help of the attacking midfielders (8 and 10). With a dismarking movement, the midfielder (8) drops down to receive and build out vertically with the other midfielder (10).

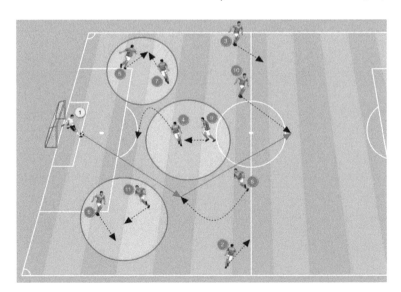

For the coach:

- Actively involve the goalkeeper in the building of the game.
- Correct body profile in an offensive direction.
- The first touch should facilitate building out from the back.
- Pay attention to the timing of the play, maintaining the correct distances between channels and occupying space in a functional and effective way.
- Preventative coverage is important: once the ball leaves the defensive zone, the centerbacks must push their line up towards the middle of the field.
- The center midfielders need to move in a coordinated and synchronized way.

3.6 BUILDING OUT FROM THE BACK AGAINST THREE OPPONENTS WHO CLOSE THE CENTERBACK'S PASSING LINES AND MARK THE DEFENSIVE MIDFIELDER

Starting the buildout from the goalkeeper (1), the two centerbacks (5 and 6) must open up, trying to "attract" the two rival attackers (9 and 11). In addition, the outside backs (2 and 3) move up to the midfield to provide width and depth. The opposing forward (9) marks our defensive midfielder (4) and the opposing winger (11) does not try to pressure, but instead covers the passing lines between the defender (6) and the attacking midfielder (8) and outside back (2) on that side. They must develop a three-vs-one in order to build out from the back and play vertically with the other attacking midfielder (10).

For the coach:

- Actively involve the goalkeeper in the building of the game.
- Correct body profile in an offensive direction.
- The first touch should facilitate building out from the back.
- Pay attention to the timing of the play, maintaining the correct distances between channels and occupying space in a functional and effective way.
- Preventative coverage is important: once the ball leaves the defensive zone, the centerbacks must push their line up towards the middle of the field.
- The center midfielders need to move in a coordinated and synchronized way.
- Encourage the outside backs to play short passes in the middle of the field.

3.7 BUILDING OUT FROM THE BACK WITH FOUR OPPONENTS WHO PRESSURE THE CENTERBACKS, THE OUTSIDE BACK, AND THE DEFENSIVE MIDFIELDER

Starting the buildout from the goalkeeper (1), the two centerbacks (5 and 6) must open up, trying to "attract" the two rival attackers (9 and 11). In addition, the outside backs (2 and 3) move up to the midfield to provide width and depth. The opposing forward (9) marks our attacking midfielder (8) and the opposing winger tries to close the passing lines to the defensive midfielder (4) and the centerback (5). The outside back on the opposite side (3) has to move forward in order to receive the ball and escape the pressure.

For the coach:

- Actively involve the goalkeeper in the building of the game.
- Correct body profile in an offensive direction.
- The first touch should facilitate building out from the back.
- Pay attention to the timing of the play, maintaining the correct distances between channels and occupying space in a functional and effective way.
- Preventative coverage is important: once the ball leaves the defensive zone, the centerbacks must push their line up towards the middle of the field.
- The center midfielders need to move in a coordinated and synchronized way.
- Train the peripheral vision of the players.

3.8 BUILDING OUT FROM THE BACK AGAINST FOUR OPPONENTS WHO PRESSURE THE CENTERBACKS AND TWO CENTER MIDFIELDERS

Starting the buildout from the goalkeeper (1), the two centerbacks (5 and 6) must open up, trying to "attract" the two rival attackers (9 and 11). In addition, the outside backs (2 and 3) move up to the midfield to provide width and depth. The opposing forward (9) marks our defensive midfielder (4) and the opposing center midfielder (10) puts pressure on our attacking midfielder (8). In this situation, the other attacking midfielder (10) has to move away with a curved movement to receive the ball on the other side of the field, moving behind the opponent (out of their view).

For the coach::

- Actively involve the goalkeeper in the building of the game.
- Correct body profile in an offensive direction.
- The first touch should facilitate building out from the back.
- Pay attention to the timing of the play, maintaining the correct distances between channels and occupying space in a functional and effective way.
- Preventative coverage is important: once the ball leaves the defensive zone, the centerbacks must push their line up towards the middle of the field.
- The center midfielders need to move in a coordinated and synchronized way.
- Train the players to dismark behind the backs of their opponents.

CHAPTER 4
ACTIVITIES

01 5 + GOALKEEPER VERSUS 2 PRESSING PLAYERS

OPERATING METHOD	Positional game

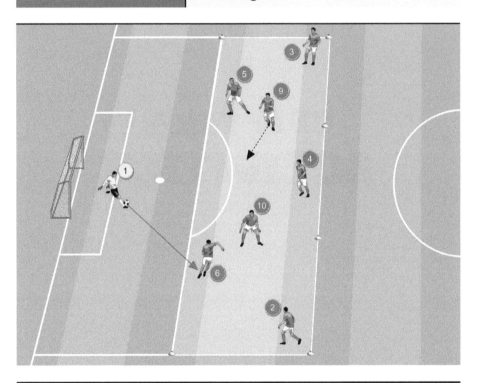

PREPARATION	OBJECTIVES	
Playing area: 40 × 30 meters. Players: 7 + 1 goalkeeper. Duration: 18 minutes. Number of series: two of 8 minutes with 1'30" of recovery between each series. Equipment: cones, two bibs, one goal, and balls.	**Team in possession:** • Dismarking • Oriented control • Keeping the ball • Passing • Mobility • Defensive transition • Occupation of space • Maintaining roles	**Team out of possession:** • Interceptions • Anticipation • Marking • Defensive Posture • Pressure • Closing passing lines • Offensive transition • Shooting on goal

ORGANIZATION

The space used for the activity is approximately double the penalty area. Use cones to form a second adjacent area of about 40×16 meters. Establish a defensive line with players in their roles, and arrange the defenders and the defensive midfielder to play against two attackers within this zone. The penalty area is only occupied by the goalkeeper, who helps keep possession and always starts the action.

DESCRIPTION

1. The action starts from the goalkeeper in a 5 + goalkeeper versus 2.
2. The team in possession has to move the ball while maintaining their positions and earns a point after completing 10 consecutive passes.
3. The defenders (Red players) must intercept the ball and finish as quickly as possible.

RULES

- The players in possession can only play within the rectangle marked out beyond the penalty area.

VARIATIONS

1. Play with two touches.
2. When the attackers recover the ball they must make at least one pass before finishing.

COACHING CONSIDERATIONS

For the players in possession:
- It's vital that the activity be carried out with a high level of intensity.
- Coach the players' first touch and body orientation towards their teammates and the play.
- Passes must be executed with the proper pace.
- Coach the technical aspects of receiving and passing.
- Maintain correct distances with proper timing while playing and dismarking.
- Get the players used to knowing where to play before receiving the ball.
- Maintain visual contact and yell "man on" or "solo" as necessary.
- In the event of losing the ball, change quickly from an offensive attitude to a defensive attitude.

For the players out of possession:
- Focus on recovering the ball.
- Close the passing lines.
- Anticipate the play.
- Carry out coordinated movements.
- Encourage offensive transitions.
- After winning the ball, change quickly from a defensive attitude to an offensive attitude.

02 7 + GOALKEEPERS VERSUS 4 PRESSING PLAYERS + 2 NEUTRALS

OPERATING METHOD	Positional game

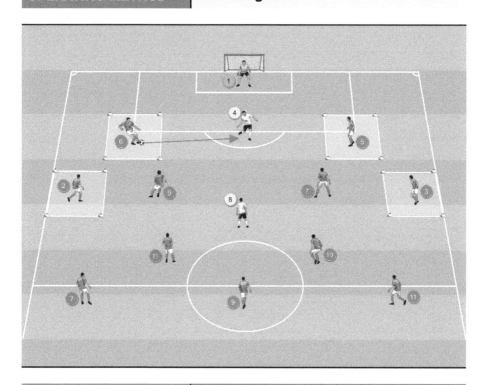

PREPARATION	OBJECTIVES	
Playing area: 60 × 50 meters. Players: 13 + 1 goalkeeper. Duration: 18 minutes. Number of series: two of 8 minutes with 1'30" of recovery between each series. Equipment: cones, six bibs (four of one color and two of another), one goal, and balls.	**Team in possession:** • Dismarking • Oriented control • Keeping the ball • Passing • Mobility • Defensive transition • Occupation of space • Maintaining roles	**Team out of possession:** • Interceptions • Anticipation • Marking • Defensive Posture • Pressure • Closing passing lines • Offensive transition • Shooting on goal

ORGANIZATION

Use the cones to create four boxes for the defenders, placing them in specific positions for building the game from the goalkeeper. Two neutrals play in the middle of the field and act as midfielders when the Blue team has the ball, and as attackers when the opponents gain possession. In the midfield, place three forwards who will play one-touch once the pressure has been broken.

DESCRIPTION

1. The action starts from the goalkeeper, with players from the team in possession lined up inside the boxes to create a situation of 4 + goalkeeper and 2 neutrals versus 4 attackers.
2. The team in possession must play out from the back while respecting the available space. The players are not allowed to leave their squares, but they can take advantage of the numerical superiority provided by the neutral players to find the three attackers located in midfield. The neutrals are the only players who are allowed to move anywhere within the playing area.
3. The team in possession scores a point after completing ten passes.
4. The four players who are not in possession must close the spaces and dispossess the opponent. Once they have stolen the ball, they can use the neutrals to finish the play as quickly as possible.

RULES

- The players in the boxes cannot leave their spaces until the ball is lost.
- The three attackers who receive the ball in midfield must play one-touch.

VARIATIONS

1. Play with two touches.
2. When the attackers recover the ball they must make at least three passes before finishing.

COACHING CONSIDERATIONS

For the players in possession:

- Maintain correct distances with proper timing while playing and dismarking.
- Get the players used to knowing where to play before receiving the ball.
- Work on the interchange between the two neutrals: when one drops down between the centerbacks, the other must do the opposite and move up between the lines.
- The players need to be able to read the situation tactically.
- The synchronization of movement between the players is important.
- Maintain visual contact and yell "man on" or "solo" as necessary.
- After losing the ball, change quickly from an offensive attitude to a defensive attitude.

For the players out of possession:

- Carry out coordinated movements.
- Encourage offensive transitions.
- After winning the ball, change quickly from a defensive attitude to an offensive attitude.

03 4 + GOALKEEPER VERSUS 4 PRESSING PLAYERS + 2 NEUTRALS

OPERATING METHOD	Positional game

PREPARATION	OBJECTIVES	
Playing area: 60 × 50 meters. Players: 10 + 1 goalkeeper. Duration: 18 minutes. Number of series: two of 8 minutes with 1'30" of recovery between each series. Equipment: cones, six bibs (four of one color and two of another), one goal, three mini-goals and balls.	Team in possession: • Dismarking • Oriented control • Keeping the ball • Passing • Mobility • Defensive transition • Numerical superiority • Occupation of space • Maintaining roles	Team out of possession: • Interceptions • Anticipation • Marking • Defensive Posture • Pressure • Closing passing lines • Offensive transition • Shooting on goal

ORGANIZATION

Organize the defensive line and start play from the goalkeeper. In the middle of the field, the two neutrals play in the role of midfielders to create a numerical superiority. The four attackers must press in order to steal the ball and finish. Once they have recovered the ball they can combine with the two neutrals to finish the action.

DESCRIPTION

1. The goalkeeper of the team in possession starts the action, creating a 4 + goalkeeper and two neutrals versus 4 attackers.
2. The team with the ball must build the game from the back to escape the opponent's pressure and score in one of the three mini-goals that are located at the midfield line.
3. The four players who are not in possession must intercept the ball, close the spaces, and dispossess the opponent. Once they have stolen the ball, they can use the neutrals to finish the play as quickly as possible.

RULES

▪ Every action starts from the goalkeeper.

VARIATIONS

1. Play with two touches.
2. When the attackers recover the ball they must make at least three passes before finishing.

COACHING CONSIDERATIONS

For the players in possession:

- Maintain correct distances with proper timing while playing and dismarking.
- Get the players used to knowing where to play before receiving the ball.
- Work on the interchange between the two neutrals: when one drops down between the centerbacks, the other must do the opposite and move up between the lines.
- The players need to be able to read the situation tactically.
- The synchronization of movement between the players is important.
- Maintain visual contact and yell "man on" or "solo" as necessary.
- After losing the ball, change quickly from an offensive attitude to a defensive attitude.

For the players out of possession:

- Carry out coordinated movements.
- Encourage offensive transitions.
- After winning the ball, change quickly from a defensive attitude to an offensive attitude.

04

7 + GOALKEEPER VERSUS 3 PRESSING PLAYERS

OPERATING METHOD	Situation

PREPARATION	OBJECTIVES	
Playing area: 60 × 70 meters. Players: 10 + 1 goalkeeper. Duration: 18 minutes. Number of series: two of 8 minutes with 1'30" of recovery between each series. Equipment: cones, three bibs, one goal, two mini-goals, and balls.	**Team in possession:** • Dismarking • Oriented control • Keeping the ball • Passing • Mobility • Vertical play • Defensive transition • Occupation of space • Maintaining roles	**Team out of possession:** • Interceptions • Anticipation • Marking • Defensive Posture • Pressure • Closing passing lines • Offensive transition • Shooting on goal

ORGANIZATION

The space used for this activity is approximately three quarters of the field. Use cones to mark out two zones between the penalty box and the midfield line (see illustration) and create a third zone from the midfield line to the two mini-goals. Arrange two centerbacks in the first zone against two pressing attackers; two midfielders in the next zone against another pressing attacker; and two outside backs who operate in the outside zones and cannot be pressed. The players out of possession must press in their respective zones. In the attacking half of the field, a midfielder must receive and lay the ball off after building out of the back before finishing.

DESCRIPTION

1. The action starts from the goalkeeper of the team in possession. There is a 2 + goalkeeper versus 2 in the first zone, and two midfielders versus a forward in the second zone. The outside backs remain in their zones and can play without being pressed. The midfielder in the offensive half must lay the ball off to one of the other two midfielders.
2. The team in possession must try to escape the pressure of the three attackers and score in one of the mini-goals. Players must remain in their zones.
3. If the ball is lost, players from the Blue team can leave their zones and transition defensively.
4. The three players out of possession must win the ball and can move anywhere to finish.

RULES

- The players from the team that is building out of the back (Blue) cannot leave their designated areas.

VARIATIONS

1. Play with two touches.
2. Deliver the ball to the outside backs in order to finish in the mini-goals.
3. When the attackers recover the ball they must make at least one pass before finishing.

COACHING CONSIDERATIONS

For the players in possession:
- Maintain correct distances with proper timing while playing and dismarking.
- Get the players used to knowing where to play before receiving the ball.
- Play with a high tempo after breaking the pressure.
- The midfielder (10) should always look to play vertically first.
- Maintain visual contact and yell "man on" or "solo" as necessary.

For the players out of possession:
- Carry out coordinated movements.

05 7 + GOALKEEPER VERSUS 3 + 1 PRESSING DEFENDER

OPERATING METHOD — Situation

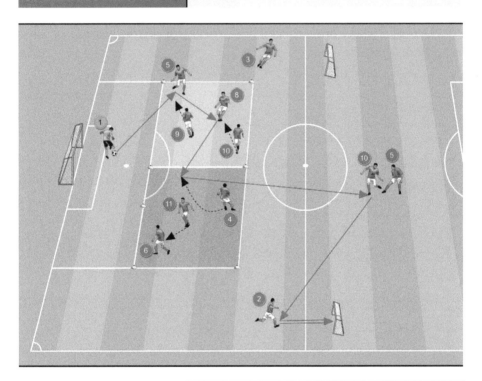

PREPARATION	OBJECTIVES	
Playing area: 60 × 70 meters. Players: 11 + 1 goalkeeper. Duration: 18 minutes. Number of series: two of 8 minutes with 1'30" of recovery between each series. Equipment: cones, four bibs, one goal, two mini-goals, and balls.	**Team in possession:** • Dismarking • Oriented control • Keeping the ball • Passing • Mobility • Vertical play • Defensive transition • Occupation of space • Maintaining roles	**Team out of possession:** • Interceptions • Anticipation • Marking • Defensive Posture • Pressure • Closing passing lines • Offensive transition • Shooting on goal

ORGANIZATION

The space used for this activity is approximately three quarters of the field. In the middle of the field, mark out a 40×16 meter rectangle in front of the penalty area and divide it in the middle as shown in the illustration (forming a double zone). Spread out the defensive line, with the centerbacks and two center midfielders inside that double zone. The third midfielder is in the other half of the field, ready to offer support.

DESCRIPTION

1. The action starts from the goalkeeper of the team in possession. A 2 + goalkeeper versus 2 attackers is created in the left zone, while there is a 2 versus 1 in the right zone.
2. A maximum of two attackers can be within either central zone as they seek to recover the ball.
3. Once Blue builds out of the back, they will look to play vertically to the third midfielder who is marked by a defender. This player must offload the ball to the outside backs to finish.
4. If the ball is lost, players from the Blue team can leave their zones and transition defensively.
5. After winning the ball, the three opponents are free to move anywhere and must finish as quickly as possible with the help of the supporting defender.

RULES

-   The players of the team building out from the back (Blue) may not leave their zones while in possession.

VARIATIONS

1. Play with two touches.
2. After the center midfielder lays the ball off, switch play and score in the mini-goal on the opposite side from where the play started.
3. When the attackers recover the ball they must make at least one pass before finishing.

COACHING CONSIDERATIONS

For the players in possession:

- Maintain correct distances with proper timing while playing and dismarking.
- Get the players used to knowing where to play before receiving the ball.
- Play with a high tempo after breaking the pressure.
- The midfielder (10) should always look to play vertically first.
- Maintain visual contact and yell "man on" or "solo" as necessary.
- Synchronize the movements of the players.
- After losing the ball, change quickly from an offensive attitude to a defensive attitude.

For the players out of possession:

- Carry out coordinated movements.

06
8 + GOALKEEPER VERSUS 4 PRESSING PLAYERS + 2 CENTERBACKS

OPERATING METHOD | Situation

PREPARATION	OBJECTIVES	
Playing area: 60 × 70 meters. Players: 14 + 1 goalkeeper. Duration: 18 minutes Number of series: two of 8 minutes with 1'30" of recovery between each series. Equipment: cones, six bibs, one goal, three mini-goals, and balls.	**Team in possession:** ▪ Dismarking ▪ Oriented control ▪ Keeping the ball ▪ Passing ▪ Mobility ▪ Vertical play ▪ Defensive transition ▪ Occupation of space ▪ Maintaining roles	**Team out of possession:** ▪ Interceptions ▪ Anticipation ▪ Marking ▪ Defensive Posture ▪ Pressure ▪ Closing passing lines ▪ Offensive transition ▪ Shooting on goal

ORGANIZATION

The space used for this activity is approximately three quarters of the field. Mark out a 40×16 meter rectangle in front of the penalty area and divide it into three zones, with the central zone wider than the others. Arrange the defensive line with the two centerbacks and two midfielders inside the central zone to create a two-vs-two. On the flanks, arrange the outside backs in one-vs-one situations. The third midfielder and the center forward in the other half of the field will, with the help of one of the two midfielders, play against two defenders and finish in one of the three mini-goals.

DESCRIPTION

1. The action starts from the goalkeeper of the team in possession, with a 2 + goalkeeper against 2 attackers situation in the central zone and one-vs-one situations in the wide zones.
2. Once Blue builds out from the back, they will look to play vertically to the third midfielder or the center forward, who are marked by two defenders. These players can combine with one of the other midfielders to finish with a three-vs-two.
3. If the ball is lost, players from the Blue team can leave their zones and transition defensively.
4. After winning the ball, the four Red opponents are free to transition offensively and may move anywhere. They must finish as quickly as possible with the help of the supporting defenders.
5. Once the attackers finish the action, start again from the goalkeeper.

RULES

- The players of the team building out (Blue) may not leave their zones while in possession.

VARIATIONS

1. Play with two touches.
2. After the layoff from the the center forward, use the two center midfielders for support.
3. When the attackers recover the ball they must make at least one pass before finishing.

COACHING CONSIDERATIONS

For the players in possession:

- Get the players used to knowing where to play before receiving the ball.
- Play with a high tempo after breaking the pressure.
- The staggered positioning and dismarking of the attackers before receiving the ball is important.
- Maintain visual contact and yell "man on" or "solo" as necessary.

For the players out of possession:

- Carry out coordinated movements.
- Encourage offensive transitions.

07 10 + GOALKEEPER VERSUS 3 PRESSING PLAYERS WITH 1 VERSUS 1 ON THE WINGS

OPERATING METHOD	Situation

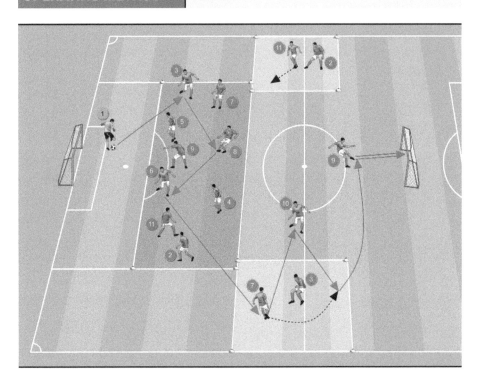

PREPARATION	OBJECTIVES	
Playing area: 60 × 70 meters. Players: 15 + 1 goalkeeper. Duration: 18 minutes. Number of series: two of 8 minutes with 1'30" of recovery between each series. Equipment: cones, five bibs, two goals, and balls.	**Team in possession:** • Dismarking • Oriented control • Keeping the ball • Passing • Mobility • Vertical play • Defensive transition • Occupation of space • Maintaining roles • Numerical superiority	**Team out of possession:** • Interceptions • Anticipation • Marking • Defensive Posture • Pressure • Closing passing lines • Offensive transition • Shooting on goal

ORGANIZATION

The space used for this activity is approximately three quarters of the field. Mark out a 40×16 meter rectangle in front of the penalty area. Create two more squares of about 20×20 meters in the wide areas at midfield. In the first zone, arrange the defensive line and two center midfielders against three opponents. In both wide zones, a wingers play against an outside back. The third midfielder and the center forward are in the other half of the field to provide support and create a two-vs-one numerical superiority when playing out on the wings; one of these players must approach while the other makes the opposite movement to finish.

DESCRIPTION

1. The action starts from the goalkeeper of the team in possession. There is a 6-vs-3 in the central area and a 1-vs-1 in each of the the wide zones.
2. The defenders and attackers must stay within their playing areas.
3. Once Blue builds out of the back, they will look to play vertically with the help of the two attackers.
4. The two forwards make opposite movements.
5. After playing in the wide zone, seek to cross to the attacker who will finish the play.
6. After winning the ball, the three Red opponents are free to transition offensively and may move anywhere. They must finish as quickly as possible with the help of the supporting defenders.
7. Once the action finishes, start again from the goalkeeper.

RULES

- The players of the team building out from the back (Blue) may not leave their zones.

VARIATIONS

1. Play with two touches.
2. After the layoff from the the center forward, use the two center midfielders for support.
3. When the attackers recover the ball they must make at least one pass before finishing.

COACHING CONSIDERATIONS

For the players in possession:

- Get the players used to knowing where to play before receiving the ball.
- Play with a high tempo after breaking the pressure.
- The staggered positioning and dismarking of the attackers before receiving the ball is important.
- Maintain visual contact and yell "man on" or "solo" as necessary.

For the players out of possession:

- Carry out coordinated movements.
- Encourage offensive transitions.

08 6 VERSUS 6 + 5 NEUTRALS WITH 2 NEUTRAL GOALKEEPERS: BUILDING THE GAME CENTRALLY

OPERATING METHOD	Situation

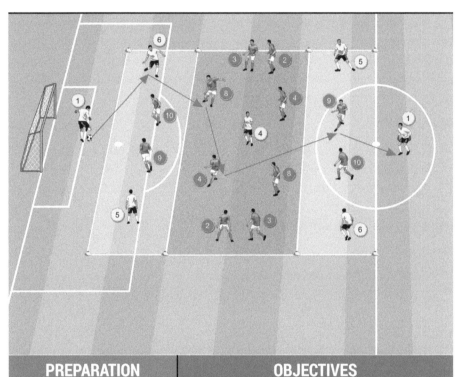

PREPARATION

Playing area: 30 × 40 meters.
Players: 17 + 2 goalkeepers.
Duration: 25 minutes.
Number of series: three of 7 minutes with 1'30" of recovery between each series.
Equipment: cones, bibs, one goal, and balls.

OBJECTIVES

Team in possession:
- Dismarking
- Oriented control
- Keeping the ball
- Passing
- Mobility
- Vertical play
- Defensive transition
- Occupation of space
- Maintaining roles
- Numerical superiority
- Geometric shapes

Team out of possession:
- Interceptions
- Anticipation
- Marking
- Defensive Posture
- Pressure
- Closing passing lines
- Offensive transition
- Shooting on goal

ORGANIZATION

The space used for this activity is approximately 30 × 40 meters. Create two zones of approximately 30 × 12 meters on each end, with a wider center zone. Divide the players into two teams of six, plus five neutral players, with two goalkeepers positioned outside the two smaller zones. The teams are arranged as shown in the illustration and either team can start with the ball.

DESCRIPTION

1. Play 6 versus 6 with 5 neutrals distributed in the different zones, plus two neutral goalkeepers in support.
2. The goalkeeper starts the action and the team in possession attempts to pass on the ground to play through the three zones and reach the opposing goalkeeper, which earns them a point.

RULES

- Players must stay within their own zones.

VARIATIONS

1. Play with two touches.
2. Recover the ball within 5 seconds or the team that won the ball earns a point.

COACHING CONSIDERATIONS

For the players in possession:
- It's vital that the activity be carried out with a high level of intensity.
- Coach the players' first touch and body orientation towards their teammates and the play.
- Passes must be executed with the proper pace.
- Coach the technical aspects of receiving and passing.
- Maintain correct distances with proper timing while playing and dismarking.
- Get the players used to knowing where to play before receiving the ball.
- The players need to be able to read the situation tactically.
- Synchronize the movements of the players.
- Attackers in staggered positions.
- Maintain visual contact and yell "man on" or "solo" as necessary.
- After losing the ball, change quickly from an offensive attitude to a defensive attitude.

For the players out of possession:
- Focus on recovering the ball.
- Close the passing lines.
- Anticipate the play.
- Carry out coordinated movements.
- Encourage offensive transitions.

09

7 VERSUS 7 + 1 NEUTRAL: BUILDING THE GAME THROUGH THE CENTERBACKS

OPERATING METHOD | Positional game

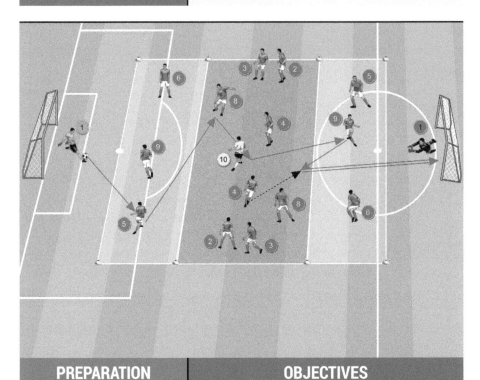

PREPARATION	OBJECTIVES	
Playing area: 30×40 meters. Players: 15 + 2 goalkeepers. Duration: 25 minutes. Number of series: three of 7 minutes with 1' 30" of recovery between each series. Equipment: cones, eight bibs (seven of one color and one of another), two goals, and balls.	**Team in possession:** ▪ Dismarking ▪ Oriented control ▪ Keeping the ball ▪ Passing ▪ Mobility ▪ Vertical play ▪ Defensive transition ▪ Occupation of space ▪ Mantaining roles ▪ Numerical superiority ▪ Geometric shapes ▪ Shooting on goal	**Team out of possession:** ▪ Interceptions ▪ Anticipation ▪ Marking ▪ Defensive Posture ▪ Pressure ▪ Closing passing lines ▪ Offensive transition

ORGANIZATION

The space used for this activity is approximately 30 × 40 meters. Create two zones of approximately 30 × 12 meters on each end, with a wider center zone. Divide the players into two teams of seven plus a neutral player and two goalkeepers who are positioned outside the two smaller zones. The teams are arranged as shown in the illustration and either team can start with the ball.

DESCRIPTION

1. Play 7 versus 7 plus one neutral player and two goalkeepers.
2. Teams must reach the opponent's defensive zone before scoring.

RULES

- Players must stay within their own zones.

VARIATIONS

1. Play with two touches.
2. Recover the ball within 5 seconds or the team that won the ball earns a point.

COACHING CONSIDERATIONS

For the players in possession:

- It's important that the activity is carried out with a high level of intensity.
- Coach the players' first touch and body orientation towards their teammates and the play.
- Passes must be executed with the proper pace.
- Coach the technical aspects of receiving and passing.
- Maintain correct distances with proper timing while playing and dismarking.
- Get the players used to knowing where to play before receiving the ball.
- The players need to be able to read the situation tactically.
- Synchronize the movements of the players.
- Attackers in staggered positions.
- Create geometric shapes.
- Defensive transitions.
- The centerback must run with the ball to attact an opponent in order to create superiorities in the middle.
- The center forward must play with their back to goal.
- Maintain visual contact and yell "man on" or "solo" as necessary.
- After losing the ball, change quickly from an offensive attitude to a defensive attitude.

For the players out of possession:

- Focus on recovering the ball.
- Close the passing lines.
- Anticipate the play.
- Carry out coordinated movements.
- Encourage offensive transitions.
- After winning the ball, change quickly from a defensive attitude to an offensive attitude.

10 6 VERSUS 6 + 2 NEUTRALS: BUILDING THE GAME THROUGH THE OUTSIDE BACK

OPERATING METHOD Positional game

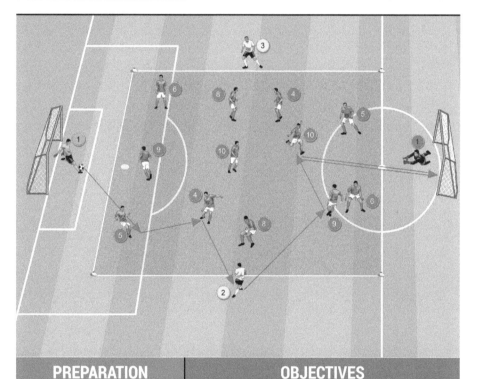

PREPARATION	OBJECTIVES	
Playing area: 30 × 40 meters. Players: 14 + 2 goalkeepers. Duration: 25 minutes Number of series: three of 7 minutes with 1'30" of recovery between each series. Equipment: cones, eight bibs (six of one color and two of another), two goals, and balls.	Team in possession: • Dismarking • Keeping the ball • Vertical play • Defensive transition • Occupation of space • Numerical superiority • Geometric shapes • Shooting on goal • Lateral play • Attracting the opponent	Team out of possession: • Interceptions • Anticipation • Marking • Defensive Posture • Pressure • Closing passing lines • Offensive transition

ORGANIZATION

The space used for this activity is approximately 30 × 40 meters. Divide the players into two teams of six players plus two neutrals who play on the sides and two goalkeepers in the goals. Either team can start with the ball.

DESCRIPTION

1. Play 6 versus 6 plus 2 neutrals and 2 goalkeepers.
2. Teams must reach the opponent's defensive zone before scoring.
3. Teams must involve the outside back when building the game from the back.

RULES

- Players must stay within their own zones.

VARIATIONS

1. Play with two touches.
2. Recover the ball within 5 seconds or the team that won the ball earns a point.

COACHING CONSIDERATIONS

For the players in possession:

- It's important that the activity is carried out with a high level of intensity.
- Coach the players' first touch and body orientation towards their teammates and the play.
- Passes must be executed with the proper pace.
- Coach the technical aspects of receiving and passing.
- Maintain correct distances with proper timing while playing and dismarking.
- Get the players used to knowing where to play before receiving the ball.
- The players need to be able to read the situation tactically.
- Synchronize the movements of the players.
- Attackers in staggered positions.
- Create geometric shapes.
- Defensive transitions.
- The centerback must run with the ball to attact an opponent in order to create superiorities in the middle.
- The neutral players must always operate behind the backs of their opponents.
- Maintain visual contact and yell "man on" or "solo" as necessary.
- After losing the ball, change quickly from an offensive attitude to a defensive attitude.

For the players out of possession:

- Focus on recovering the ball.
- Close the passing lines.
- Anticipate the play.
- Carry out coordinated movements.
- Encourage offensive transitions.
- After winning the ball, change rapidly from a defensive attitude to an offensive attitude.

11 4 VERSUS 4 + 4 NEUTRALS WITH ONE NEUTRAL GOALKEEPER: FORWARD RUN FROM THE THIRD MAN

OPERATING METHOD	Positional game

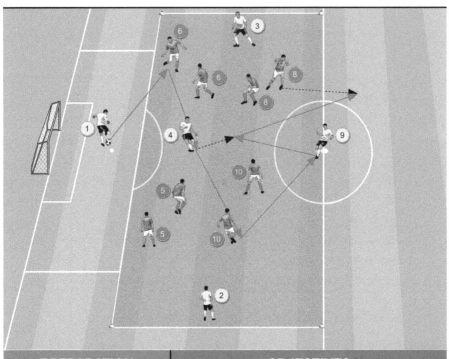

PREPARATION	OBJECTIVES	
Playing area: 45 × 35 meters. Players: 12 + 1 goalkeeper. Duration: 21 minutes. Number of series: three of 6 minutes with 1'30" of recovery between each series. Equipment: cones, nine bibs (five of one color and four of another), one goal, and balls.	**Team in possession:** ▪ Dismarking ▪ Oriented control ▪ Keeping the ball ▪ Passing ▪ Mobility ▪ Vertical play ▪ Defensive transition ▪ Occupation of space ▪ Maintaining roles ▪ Numerical superiority ▪ Geometric shapes	**Team out of possession:** ▪ Interceptions ▪ Anticipation ▪ Marking ▪ Defensive Posture ▪ Pressure ▪ Closing passing lines ▪ Offensive transition

ORGANIZATION

The playing area for the activity is approximately 45 × 35 meters. Divide the players into two teams of eight, plus four neutrals and the goalkeeper, who starts with the ball.

DESCRIPTION

1. Play 4 versus 4 with a goalkeeper and 4 neutrals arranged within the zone. The goal is to get the ball over the end line.
2. The goalkeeper starts the action.
3. A 4-3-1 is created with the neutrals acting as the outside backs, defensive center midfielder, and striker.
4. Attack the spaces with passes on the ground, exploiting the numerical superiority provided by the neutrals.
5. All the neutral players must touch the ball before advancing over the line.
6. The attacking neutral up front plays with their back to goal to facilitate forward runs from the midfielders.

RULES

- The players must respect their roles.
- The goalkeepers can only play with their feet.
- The team that makes the most forward runs wins.

VARIATIONS

1. Play with two touches.
2. Recover the ball within 5 seconds or the team that won the ball earns a point.

COACHING CONSIDERATIONS

For the players in possession:
- It's important that the activity is carried out with a high level of intensity.
- Coach the players' first touch and body orientation towards their teammates and the play.
- Passes must be executed with the proper pace.
- Coach the technical aspects of receiving and passing.
- Maintain correct distances with proper timing while playing and dismarking.
- Get the players used to knowing where to play before receiving the ball.
- Attack with players in staggered positions and combine with one-twos.
- Forward runs from the third man.
- Maintain visual contact and yell "man on" or "solo" as necessary.
- Shots on goal must be carried out first-time and with power.
- After losing the ball, change quickly from an offensive attitude to a defensive attitude.

For the players out of possession:
- Close the passing lines.
- Anticipate the play.
- Carry out coordinated movements.
- Encourage offensive transitions.
- After winning the ball, change rapidly from a defensive attitude to an offensive attitude.

12 8 VS 8 + GOALKEEPERS: ATTACKING THE SPACE BEHIND THE DEFENSIVE LINE

OPERATING METHOD	Thematic game

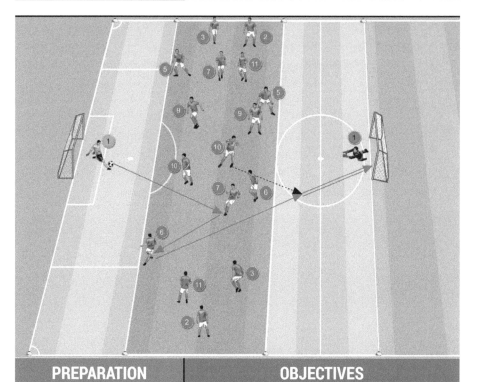

PREPARATION	OBJECTIVES	
Playing area: 60 × 70 meters. Players: 16 + 2 goalkeepers. Duration: 18 minutes. Number of series: two of 8 minutes with 1'30" of recovery between each series. Equipment: cones, eight bibs, two goals, and balls.	**Team in possession:** • Dismarking • Oriented control • Keeping the ball • Passing • Mobility • Vertical play • Defensive transition • Occupation of space • Maintaining roles • Direct Attacking • Diagonal Movements	**Team out of possession:** • Interceptions • Anticipation • Marking • Defensive Posture • Pressure • Closing passing lines • Offensive transition • Shooting on goal

ORGANIZATION

Mark out a playing area that extends past the center circle and divide it into three zones, with the central zone approximately 60x30 meters and two smaller end-zones. Divide the players into two teams of eight and arrange them in the central zone.

DESCRIPTION

1. The action starts from the goalkeeper, in a 4-1-3 formation.
2. Play within the central area until the opponent's defensive line is overcome. Once this happens, one additional teammate can go to help the attacker.
3. Make diagonal movements to look for through-balls.

RULES

- Players should operate in the spaces associated with their roles.

VARIATIONS

1. Play with two touches.
2. Push up a third attacker after overcoming the defensive line.
3. When the opponent wins the ball they must make at least one pass before finishing.

COACHING CONSIDERATIONS

For the players in possession:

- It's important that the activity is carried out with a high level of intensity.
- Coach the players' first touch and body orientation towards their teammates and the play.
- Passes must be executed with the proper pace.
- Coach the technical aspects of receiving and passing.
- Maintain correct distances with proper timing while playing and dismarking.
- Get the players used to knowing where to play before receiving the ball.
- Play with a high tempo after breaking the pressure.
- The players need to be able to read the situation tactically.
- Encourage cutting movements.
- Maintain visual contact and yell "man on" or "solo" as necessary.
- Encourage one-twos and external and internal triangulations.
- After losing the ball, change quickly from an offensive attitude to a defensive attitude.

For the players out of possession:

- Close the passing lines.
- Anticipate the play.
- Close the spaces.
- Carry out coordinated movements.
- Encourage offensive transitions.
- After winning the ball, change rapidly from a defensive attitude to an offensive attitude.

13 8 VERSUS 8 + GOALKEEPER: BUILDING FROM THE BACK WHILE MAINTAINING ROLES IN A SPECIFIC SPACE

OPERATING METHOD	Thematic game

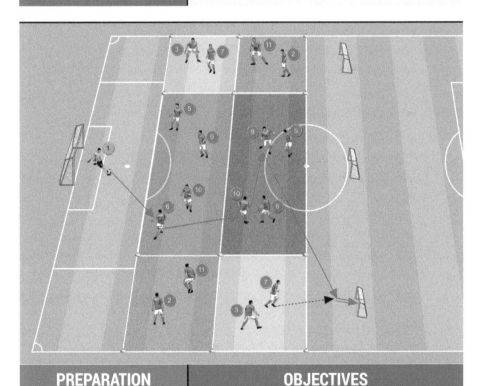

PREPARATION	OBJECTIVES	
Playing area: 60 × 70 meters. Players: 16 + 1 goalkeeper. Duration: 18 minutes. Number of series: two of 8 minutes with 1'30" of recovery between each series. Equipment: cones, eight bibs, one goal, three mini-goals, and balls.	**Team in possession:** • Dismarking • Oriented control • Keeping the ball • Passing • Mobility • Vertical play • Defensive transition • Occupation of space • Maintaining roles • Direct Attacking • Diagonal Movements	**Team out of possession:** • Interceptions • Anticipation • Marking • Defensive Posture • Pressure • Closing passing lines • Offensive transition • Shooting on goal

ORGANIZATION

Divide the space from the edge of the penalty area to the midfield line into six zones, with the two central zones being the largest. Separate the players into two teams of eight. Place one player from each team in each wide zone, with two players from each team in the two middle zones. Set up three mini-goals as in the illustration.

DESCRIPTION

1. Start the action from the goalkeeper in a 4-4 formation.
2. The team in possession must build out while respecting their own spaces and finish in one of the three mini-goals located in midfield.
3. Try to get behind the opponent's back line.
4. Play 2 versus 2 in the central zones and one versus one in the wide zones.
5. Make diagonal movements to look for through-balls.

RULES

- Players should operate in the spaces associated with their roles.

VARIATIONS

1. Play with two touches.
2. When the opponent wins the ball they must make at least one pass before finishing.

COACHING CONSIDERATIONS

For the players in possession:
- It's important that the activity is carried out with a high level of intensity.
- Coach the players' first touch and body orientation towards their teammates and the play.
- Passes must be executed with the proper pace.
- Coach the technical aspects of receiving and passing.
- Maintain correct distances with proper timing while playing and dismarking.
- Get the players used to knowing where to play before receiving the ball.
- Play with a high tempo after breaking the pressure.
- The players need to be able to read the situation tactically.
- Encourage cutting movements.
- Maintain visual contact and yell "man on" or "solo" as necessary.
- Encourage one-twos and external and internal triangulations.
- After losing the ball, change quickly from an offensive attitude to a defensive attitude.

For the players out of possession:
- Close the passing lines and spaces.
- Anticipate the play.
- Carry out coordinated movements.
- Encourage offensive transitions.
- After winning the ball, change quickly from a defensive attitude to an offensive attitude.

14 10 VERSUS 10 + GOALKEEPER: SEEKING SUPERIORITY THROUGH AN ADVANCING CENTERBACK

OPERATING METHOD	Thematic game

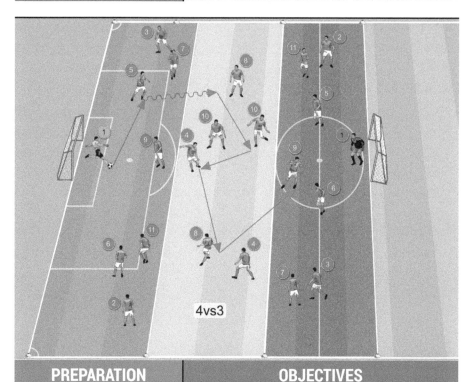

4vs3

PREPARATION

Playing area: 60 × 70 meters.
Players: 20 + 2 goalkeepers.
Duration: 23 minutes.
Number of series: two of 10 minutes with 1'30" of recovery in between.
Equipment: cones, ten bibs, two goals, and balls.

OBJECTIVES

Team in possession:
- Dismarking
- Oriented control
- Keeping the ball
- Passing
- Mobility
- Vertical play
- Defensive transition
- Occupation of space
- Maintaining roles
- Direct Attacking
- Diagonal Movements
- Shooting on goal

Team out of possession:
- Interceptions
- Anticipation
- Marking
- Defensive Posture
- Pressure
- Closing passing lines
- Offensive transition
- Shooting on goal

ORGANIZATION

Mark out a playing area that extends past the center circle and divide it into three zones. Organize two teams of ten players plus goalkeepers as shown in the illustration.

DESCRIPTION

1. The action starts from the goalkeepers, with both teams in 4-2-3-1 formations.
2. The team in possession must build out by looking to create a superiority through the advance of a centerback. This will create a 4 versus 3 in the middle of the field.
3. Players should try to score goals from their respective zones.
4. Only one of the centerbacks can move up into the central zone.
5. Play 4 versus 3 in the first zone when building out.
6. Play 3 versus 3 in the central zone (4 versus 3 when a centerback moves up).
7. Play 3 versus 4 in the third zone.

RULES

- Players should operate in the spaces associated with their roles.

VARIATIONS

1. Play with two touches.
2. When the opponent wins the ball they must make at least one pass before finishing.

COACHING CONSIDERATIONS

For the players in possession:
- It's important that the activity is carried out with a high level of intensity.
- Coach the players' first touch and body orientation towards their teammates and the play.
- Passes must be executed with the proper pace.
- Coach the technical aspects of receiving and passing.
- Maintain correct distances with proper timing while playing and dismarking.
- Get the players used to knowing where to play before receiving the ball.
- Play with a high tempo after breaking the pressure.
- The players need to be able to read the situation tactically.
- Maintain visual contact and yell "man on" or "solo" as necessary.
- Encourage the centerback to "target" an opponent to attract in order to achieve numerical superiority in the middle of the field.
- After losing the ball, change quickly from an offensive attitude to a defensive attitude.

For the players out of possession:
- Close the passing lines and spaces.
- Anticipate the play.
- Carry out coordinated movements.
- Encourage offensive transitions.
- After winning the ball, change rapidly from a defensive attitude to an offensive attitude.

15 10 VERSUS 10 + GOALKEEPER: SEEKING NUMERICAL SUPERIORITY IN THE WIDE CHANNELS

OPERATING METHOD	Thematic game

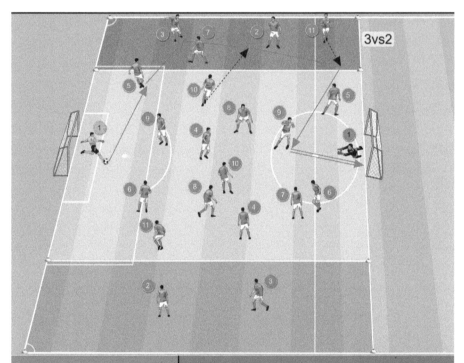

3vs2

PREPARATION

Playing area: 60 × 70 meters.
Players: 20 + 2 goalkeepers.
Duration: 22 minutes.
Number of series: two of 10 minutes with 1'30" of recovery in between.
Equipment: cones, ten bibs, two goals, and balls.

OBJECTIVES

Team in possession:
- Dismarking
- Oriented control
- Keeping the ball
- Passing
- Mobility
- Vertical play
- Defensive transition
- Occupation of space
- Maintaining roles
- Direct Attacking
- Diagonal Movements
- Shooting on goal

Team out of possession:
- Interceptions
- Anticipation
- Marking
- Defensive Posture
- Pressure
- Closing passing lines
- Offensive transition
- Shooting on goal

ORGANIZATION

Mark out a playing area that extends past the center circle and divide it into three zones. The wide channels should measure approximately 60 × 15 meters each. Divide the players into two teams of ten plus goalkeepers.

DESCRIPTION

1. The action starts from the goalkeeper, with both teams in 4-2-3-1 formations.
2. Only the wide players from either team (2, 3, 7 and 11) plus one midfielder from the team in possession can enter the outside channels.
3. The team in possession must build out by looking for superiorities in the wide channels.
4. Play 2 versus 2 in the wide channels (3 versus 2 when a center midfielder moves out wide).

RULES

▪ Players should operate in the spaces associated with their roles.

VARIATIONS

1. Play with two touches.
2. When the opponent wins the ball they must make at least one pass before finishing.

COACHING CONSIDERATIONS

For the players in possession:
- It's important that the activity is carried out with a high level of intensity.
- Coach the players' first touch and body orientation towards their teammates and the play.
- Passes must be executed with the proper pace.
- Coach the technical aspects of receiving and passing.
- Maintain correct distances with proper timing while playing and dismarking.
- Get the players used to knowing where to play before receiving the ball.
- Play with a high tempo after breaking the pressure.
- The players need to be able to read the situation tactically.
- Maintain visual contact and yell "man on" or "solo" as necessary.
- Encourage numerical advantages in the wide channels.
- After losing the ball, change quickly from an offensive attitude to a defensive attitude.

For the players out of possession:
- Close the passing lines and spaces.
- Anticipate the play.
- Carry out coordinated movements.
- Encourage offensive transitions.
- After winning the ball, change rapidly from a defensive attitude to an offensive attitude.

16 10 VERSUS 8 + GOALKEEPER: CIRCULATING THE BALL TO BUILD THE GAME WITH THE OUTSIDE BACKS

OPERATING METHOD	Developing the game

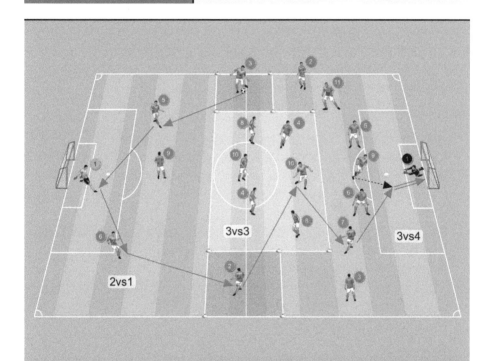

PREPARATION	OBJECTIVES	
Playing area: 60 × 100 meters. Players: 18 + 2 goalkeepers. Duration: 22 minutes. Number of series: two of 10 minutes with 1'30" of recovery in between. Equipment: cones, eight bibs, two goals, and balls.	**Team in possession:** ■ Dismarking ■ Oriented control ■ Keeping the ball ■ Passing ■ Mobility ■ Vertical play ■ Defensive transition ■ Occupation of space ■ Maintaining roles ■ Direct Attacking ■ Diagonal Movements ■ Shooting on goal	**Team out of possession:** ■ Interceptions ■ Anticipation ■ Marking ■ Defensive Posture ■ Pressure ■ Closing passing lines ■ Offensive transition ■ Shooting on goal

ORGANIZATION

Use the entire field. Divide the players into two teams; one in a 4-2-3-1 formation and the other with eight players plus a goalkeeper playing in a 4-2-1-1. In the midfield, set up two 20 x 20 meter squares out wide with a zone measuring approximately 40 × 30 meters in the center.

DESCRIPTION

1. The action starts with the goalkeeper, in a 4-2-3-1 formation.
2. The team in possession begins the buildout with a 2 versus 1 + the goalkeeper.
3. Look to switch play during the buildout in order to disorganize the opponent. One of the outside backs should help the buildout when appropriate, and cannot be pressured within their playing space.
4. Play 3 versus 3 in the middle zone. One of the center midfielders must receive from the outside back before looking for the forwards.
5. Play with a 3 versus 4 in the finishing zone.
6. When possession is lost, the opposing team can score freely and both teams can play without restrictions until the sequence is finished. Afterwards, restart play from the Blue goalkeeper.

RULES

- Players should operate in the spaces associated with their roles.

VARIATIONS

1. Play with two touches.
2. When the opponent wins the ball they must make at least one pass before finishing.

COACHING CONSIDERATIONS

For the players in possession:

- Coach the players' first touch and body orientation towards their teammates and the play.
- Maintain correct distances with proper timing while playing and dismarking.
- Get the players used to knowing where to play before receiving the ball.
- Play with a high tempo after breaking the pressure.
- The players need to be able to read the situation tactically.
- Maintain visual contact and yell "man on" or "solo" as necessary.
- Encourage switches of play.
- After losing the ball, change quickly from an offensive attitude to a defensive attitude.

For the players out of possession:

- Close the passing lines and spaces.
- Carry out coordinated movements.
- Encourage offensive transitions.
- After winning the ball, change rapidly from a defensive attitude to an offensive attitude.

17 10 VERSUS 10 + GOALKEEPER: BUILDING THE GAME WITH VERTICAL CHANNELS

OPERATING METHOD	Thematic game

PREPARATION	OBJECTIVES	
Playing area: 60 × 70 meters. Players: 20 + 2 goalkeepers. Duration: 22 minutes. Number of series: two of 10 minutes with 1' 30'' of recovery in between. Equipment: cones, ten bibs, two goals, and balls	**Team in possession:** ▪ Dismarking ▪ Oriented control ▪ Keeping the ball ▪ Passing ▪ Mobility ▪ Vertical play ▪ Defensive transition ▪ Occupation of space ▪ Maintaining roles ▪ Direct Attacking ▪ Diagonal Movements ▪ Shooting on goal	**Team out of possession:** ▪ Interceptions ▪ Anticipation ▪ Marking ▪ Defensive Posture ▪ Pressure ▪ Closing passing lines ▪ Offensive transition ▪ Shooting on goal

ORGANIZATION

Mark out a space of about 60 × 70 meters and divide it into five channels, with external zones that measure approximately 10 × 70 meters and a central channel that measures 30 × 70 meters. Divide the players into two teams of ten + goalkeepers. Arrange the players as shown in the illustration.

DESCRIPTION

1. The action starts from the goalkeeper, in a 4-2-3-1 formation.
2. During the buildout phase (only in this moment) the outside back and winger must be in different channels.
3. Play 6 versus 6 in the central channel.
4. On the wings, 3 and 11 (on the left) and 2 and 7 (on the right) must play in their assigned channels.
5. If the team in possession loses the ball they will transition defensively and can leave their zones.
6. When a team takes possession of the ball they must organize themselves in their assigned zones.
7. When in possession, the players must respect their assigned channels and zones.
8. When out of possession, the players are free to move about the field.
9. The other players can move in the central channel.
10. The players can only score from their assigned zones.

RULES

- Players should operate in the spaces associated with their roles.
- The team that scores the most goals wins.

VARIATIONS

1. Play with two touches.
2. When the opponent wins the ball, they must make at least one pass before finishing.

COACHING CONSIDERATIONS

For the players in possession:
- Maintain correct distances with proper timing while playing and dismarking.
- Get the players used to knowing where to play before receiving the ball.
- Play with a high tempo after breaking the pressure.
- The players need to be able to read the situation tactically.
- Maintain visual contact and yell "man on" or "solo" as necessary.
- Create passing lines to develop the play.
- After losing the ball, change quickly from an offensive attitude to a defensive attitude.

For the players out of possession:
- Carry out coordinated movements.
- Encourage offensive transitions.
- After winning the ball, change rapidly from a defensive attitude to an offensive attitude.

18

7 + GOALKEEPER VERSUS 6: BUILDING THE GAME LONG IN THE CENTRAL ZONE

OPERATING METHOD   Developing the game

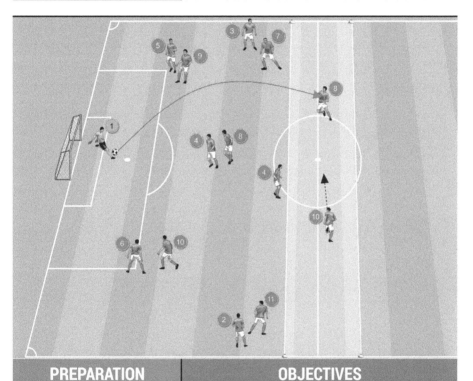

PREPARATION

Playing area: **60 × 50 meters.**
Players: **13 + 1 goalkeeper.**
Duration: **18 minutes.**
Number of series: **two of 8 minutes with 1'30" of recovery between each series.**
Equipment: **cones, six bibs, one goal, and balls.**

OBJECTIVES

Team in possession:
- Dismarking
- Oriented control
- Keeping the ball
- Passing
- Mobility
- Vertical play
- Defensive transition
- Occupation of space
- Maintaining roles

Team out of possession:
- Interceptions
- Anticipation
- Marking
- Defensive Posture
- Pressure
- Closing passing lines
- Offensive transition
- Shooting on goal

ORGANIZATION

On half a field, a team of 7 plays in a 4-1-2 formation and the other six players are free to move as they wish. Use cones to mark out a 15x60 meter zone at the midfield line, where two players are located.

DESCRIPTION

1. The action starts with the goalkeeper, who must look to build out through the two center midfielders located within the midfield zone.
2. Once the ball arrives, the midfielders must try to keep possession by making 10 consecutive passes with their teammates.
3. The two midfielders must distance themselves within this zone (only they can exploit this space) and cannot pass the ball to one another. They are only allowed to combine with players from the first zone.
4. If the opponents recover the ball, they attempt to score against the back line plus one midfielder.
5. Once the action is finished, the goalkeeper restarts the play.

RULES

- Every action starts from the goalkeeper.

VARIATIONS

1. Play with two touches.
2. When the opponent wins the ball they must make at least three passes before finishing.

COACHING CONSIDERATIONS

For the players in possession:
- It's important that the activity is carried out with a high level of intensity.
- Coach the players' first touch and body orientation towards their teammates and the play.
- Coach the technical aspects of receiving and passing.
- Maintain correct distances with proper timing while playing and dismarking.
- Get the players used to knowing where to play before receiving the ball.
- The players need to be able to read the situation tactically.
- Synchronize the movements of the players.
- Attack through long balls.
- Maintain visual contact and yell "man on" or "solo" as necessary.
- After losing the ball, change quickly from an offensive attitude to a defensive attitude.

For the players out of possession:
- Focus on recovering the ball.
- Close the passing lines.
- Anticipate the play.
- Encourage offensive transitions.
- After winning the ball, change rapidly from a defensive attitude to an offensive attitude.

19 10 VERSUS 7 + GOALKEEPER: BUILDING THE GAME LONG THROUGH THE WINGERS

OPERATING METHOD	Developing the game

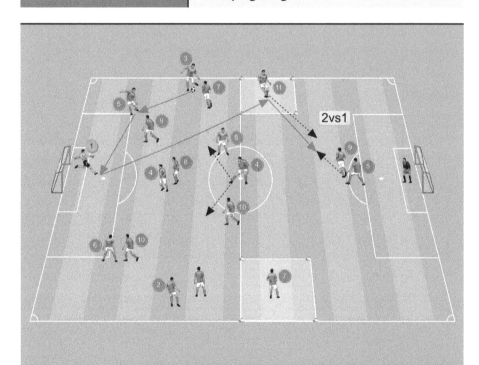

PREPARATION	OBJECTIVES	
Playing area: 60 × 100 meters. Players: 17 + 2 goalkeepers. Duration: 18 minutes. Number of series: two of 8 minutes with 1'30" of recovery between each series. Equipment: cones, six bibs, two goals, and balls.	**Team in possession:** ▪ Dismarking ▪ Oriented control ▪ Keeping the ball ▪ Passing ▪ Mobility ▪ Vertical play ▪ Defensive transition ▪ Occupation of space ▪ Maintaining roles	**Team out of possession:** ▪ Interceptions ▪ Anticipation ▪ Marking ▪ Defensive Posture ▪ Pressure ▪ Closing passing lines ▪ Offensive transition ▪ Shooting on goal

ORGANIZATION

In one half the field, a team of seven builds out in a 4-2-1 formation against six opponents who are free to move as they wish. In the other half, organize one attacker and one defender, and mark out ten 10 meter squares on each sideline with an attacker in each.

DESCRIPTION

1. The action starts from the goalkeeper who, under pressure from the opponent, must look to build out long through the two attackers who are inside the boxes on the other side of the field.
2. After reaching a winger with the long buildout, the forward must approach to help by creating a 2 versus 1.
3. If the opponents recover the ball, they should try to score, developing the play in a 6 versus 7.
4. If the defender wins the 2 versus 1, the play is over.
5. Once the sequence is finished, the goalkeeper restarts the action.

RULES

- Every action starts from the goalkeeper.

VARIATIONS

1. Play with two touches.
2. When the opponent wins the ball they must make at least one pass before finishing.

COACHING CONSIDERATIONS

For the players in possession:

- It's important that the activity is carried out with a high level of intensity.
- Coach the players' first touch and body orientation towards their teammates and the play.
- Coach the technical aspects of receiving and passing.
- Maintain correct distances with proper timing while playing and dismarking.
- Get the players used to knowing where to play before receiving the ball.
- The players need to be able to read the situation tactically.
- Synchronize the movements of the players.
- Attack through long balls.
- Maintain visual contact and yell "man on" or "solo" as necessary.
- After losing the ball, change quickly from an offensive attitude to a defensive attitude.

For the players out of possession:

- Focus on recovering the ball.
- Close the passing lines.
- Anticipate the play.
- Encourage offensive transitions.
- After winning the ball, change quickly from a defensive attitude to an offensive attitude.

20 10 VERSUS 10 + GOALKEEPER: BUILDING THE GAME LONG BY SKIPPING THE MIDFIELD

OPERATING METHOD	Thematic game

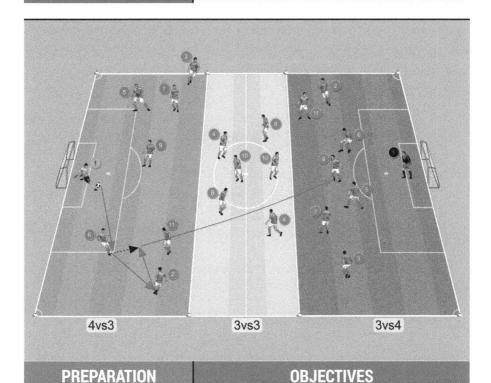

4vs3   3vs3   3vs4

PREPARATION	OBJECTIVES	
Playing area: 60 × 100 meters. Players: 20 + 2 goalkeepers. Duration: 18 minutes. Number of series: two of 8 minutes with 1'30" of recovery between each series. Equipment: cones, ten bibs, two goals, and balls.	**Team in possession:** • Dismarking • Oriented control • Keeping the ball • Passing • Mobility • Vertical play • Defensive transition • Occupation of space • Maintaining roles • Shooting on goal • Attacking the second ball	**Team out of possession:** • Interceptions • Anticipation • Marking • Defensive Posture • Pressure • Closing passing lines • Offensive transition • Shooting on goal

ORGANIZATION

Divide the field into three areas: playing 4 versus 3 in the building of the game zone, 3 versus 3 in the consolidation zone (in a space of approximately 20 x 60 meters), and 3 versus 4 in the finishing zone.

DESCRIPTION

1. The action starts from the goalkeeper, and the attacking team must move the ball with the help of the midfielders, who may only lay the ball off and cannot play vertically.
2. Under pressure from the opponent, the team in possession must look to build the game long, skipping the consolidation space and going directly to the finishing zone.
3. After reaching the finishing zone, play with 3 + one supporting midfielder versus 4.
4. Once the sequence is finished, start again from the opposite goalkeeper.

RULES

- Every action starts from the goalkeeper.

VARIATIONS

1. Allow two midfielders to move up into the finishing zone.
2. Play with two touches.

COACHING CONSIDERATIONS

For the players in possession:

- It's important that the activity is carried out with high intensity.
- Coach the players' first touch and body orientation towards their teammates and the play.
- Coach the technical aspects of receiving and passing.
- Maintain correct distances with proper timing while playing and dismarking.
- Get the players used to knowing where to play before receiving the ball.
- The players need to be able to read the situation tactically.
- Synchronize the movements of the players.
- Attack through long balls.
- Maintain visual contact and yell "man on" or "solo" as necessary.
- Numerical superiority.
- After losing the ball, change quickly from an offensive attitude to a defensive attitude.

For the players out of possession:

- Focus on recovering the ball.
- Close the passing lines.
- Anticipate the play.
- Encourage offensive transitions.
- After winning the ball, change quickly from a defensive attitude to an offensive attitude.

CONCLUSIONS

Football has grown a lot at a tactical level in recent years, especially in Europe. I think that outlining a game model adapted to the type of players that we train is essential for their growth.

Building from the back has the objective of "attracting opponents", or moving the other team's center of gravity to where we believe it is weakest, in order to attack them effectively through coordinated movements. With controlled possession of the ball, we will seek out the correct action for attacking the opponent's defensive line.

I propose there always be a transition phase in every situation, as I think it's no longer enough to just train one phase at a time and separate it from the rest of the game. Therefore, in these activities I try to recreate a dynamic flow that resembles a real match situation as closely as possible.

I think that we lose focus when we consider the player as an individual who is separate from the group, because in the game they will be placed in a context of continuous flow and constant interactions with their teammates and opponents. For me, the individual's value within the collective game is strengthened by creating smart players who can think and play football.

It is the players themselves who can recognize their own behaviors and tendencies, and for this reason it's essential that the training sessions focus on their skills. I believe that coaches should not find solutions for their players, but simply inspire them to develop their own ideas in order to make the game more "natural", and therefore freer.

ABOUT THE AUTHOR

Davide Zenorini
UEFA B licensed coach

Davide Zenorini (born in 1980) is a UEFA B licensed coach.

In recent years he has worked as a youth coach for Vicenza Calcio before moving to the Primavera category and the first team, where he served in the role of assistant coach and match analyst.

After playing in the youth categories of FC Inter and Calcio Padova, he stopped playing football at an early age. After ending his playing carrer, he graduated in stage design, lived abroad, and began his development as a coach. To achieve this last goal, he decided to study the different methods of Europe's best clubs by visiting Inter, Ajax, Barcelona, and Bayern Munich, among others.

For several years he has also managed the top level of Altovicentino (Clubs in Serie D and Inter Training Center) and has participated in several summer camps, including the FC Inter Camp. In addition, he took the SICS course in Coverciano, to train as an analyst.

Lightning Source UK Ltd.
Milton Keynes UK
UKHW051046270223
417719UK00011B/115